Adam Ditchburn

As the Crow Flies
And Other Poems

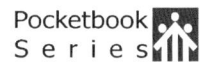

Don Bosco Publications

Pocketbook Series

Don Bosco Publications
Thornleigh House, Sharples Park, Bolton BL1 6PQ
United Kingdom

ISBN 978-1-909080-43-0
©Don Bosco Publications, 2019
©Adam Ditchburn

All rights reserved. No part of this publication may be reproduced, stored in a retrieval system or transmitted in any form or by any means without the prior permission in writing of Don Bosco Publications. Enquiries concerning reproduction and requests for permissions should be sent to The Manager, Don Bosco Publications, at the address above.

Front cover photo by Adam Ditchburn, 2019

Printed in Great Britain by Jump Design and Print

Contents

Introduction 5

As the Crow Flies 7

The Boy with a Wolf for a Heart 9

Whisper 11

Woke 13

When I was Seventeen 15

Lanzarote at Easter 17

A Day at the British Library 20

The Insignificance of Mistletoe 22

The Mess of Tomorrow 23

A London Sonnet 25

Humber Bridge 26

Virginia's Walk	28
Mirrors	30
Find Me	32
Saharan Sand	34
Tiki Bar on Fernandina	36
Until I Die	38
Shard	39
Alarm	40
Wildflower	41
Cord	43
Next Year	44
Museum Assistant on Opening Night	45
Merlot	47
Refugee	48
The Silence	50
About the Author	53

Introduction

My first collection of poetry to be published, 'As the Crow Flies', contains a variety of themes and threads. The poems also vary in style, sophistication and subject matter, which I hope reflects the ever-growing nature of my writing voice. The contents of this collection cover my reflections on life, death and the afterlife at their deepest level on one hand, while laughing about the experience of flying on a budget airline or the opening night of a museum exhibition on the other.

The reading of poetry is a subjective activity and one which is different for each individual, some poems are better read in silence, whereas others really need to be read aloud; I'll leave you, the reader, to decide which is which.

I'd like to thank everyone who has supported and continues to support my journey as a writer, particularly my family and friends who are a never-ending inspiration. I'd also like to thank Don Bosco Publications for producing this book of poetry, which I know is a new direction for them. This book is dedicated to the memory of my wonderful Nanna, Jane Taylor, the bravest person I ever knew; you are always with me, alive in the flight of the crow.

Adam Ditchburn
Swanland, Yorkshire, 2019

Instagram @adamandthemuses
Twitter @adamandthemuses
Facebook.com/adamandthemuses

As the Crow Flies

I'm glad you met my children
I wish you could've stayed
to watch them grow.
I sing your lullaby to them
as you soar above us;
alive in the flight of the crow.

Is it childish to speak of
the unfairness of death?
How it snatched you away?
I listen for your answer in the bird's
caw. I can hear your voice
but don't understand what you say.

I hold your hand as the outro
approaches, and your eyes say

"even the strongest song dies."
A tap at the window, a beak
on the glass, I watch through
salted rivers, as the crow flies.

The Boy with a Wolf for a Heart

I am the boy with a wolf for a heart; always howling, hunting for something, someone.

In echoes and dreams of echoes and echoes of dreams,
I run through grass and gravel.
I feel the breeze from the North Sea and
taste the salt it gifts to my lips.
I hear thunder on Thursdays,
chase rainbows on Fridays;
until the rainbows are moved from my reach.

I step into the dark; not blinking, barely breathing.
Filled with anxiety and strain, emotional blackmail
hanging over my frame

and my heart still hunting, howling
for something, someone.

Can there be a quiet time for us all?
A certain hour of the day when everyone
shuts up and sleeps.
A certain hour of the day when the church mouse
can creep to wherever she creeps; unhindered.
I wonder if there can. If there can, I'll sit and
sing silently. How can I exist without a song?

A silent song is still a song.
And in my silent song
my heart will be hunting,
howling for something, someone.

Whisper

I don't always smile
but I always smile in the forest.
There the trees have eyes and
the leaves have songs, the birds
share stories and the dead
whisper in the breeze.

It was there we first kissed,
once upon a broken night.
There our eyes were hungry
and our hearts ran wild, nobody
was watching and the dead slept
beneath our feet.

12

I swore I'd love you forever
and forever seemed less than a word.
There we were young lovers and
our brains were not full. We were
invincible and the dead were
confined to history.

Woke

We walked on cobbled colonisation
beneath Spanish moss on Saturday.
In sunshine that kissed us, and woke us;
from lonely songs,
winter walks and
campfire talks.

We were surrounded by dusty graves
beneath Spanish moss on Saturday.
History said you and I have been blessed;
the masters of the world,
owners of slaves,
now we're ashamed.

We are the causers,
the abhorrent enforcers.

14

The men who wrote "the truth".
We closed our eyes
and drifted softly to sleep
beneath Spanish moss on Saturday.

When I was Seventeen

I see those beautiful young men
looking down their noses at me.
They're busy being all the things
I know I could have been,
if I'd been a little braver;
when I was seventeen.

Once I laughed, the way they laugh at me
behind those unwrinkled smiles.
I'm busy mourning all the things
that could've, should've been,
if I'd been a little surer;
when I was seventeen.

16

When I was seventeen, oh
the places and the people I'd never been.
It was all waiting for me
if I'd dared to make a dream,
more than a dream.
When I was seventeen.

Lanzarote at Easter

This Irish plane will be full of
overweight English and
over-mouthy Scots.
When I get there, I'll
probably be knocked down
by a maniac on a mobility scooter.

I'm sure the person sitting
next to me will be
reading *The Scum*.
I'll look disapprovingly
as I put on my noise reduction
headphones and blackout glasses.

As I take my seat, I'm hit
by a wave of
lager burps.
Handkerchief to my nose,
sprayed with
L'Eau d'Issey Majeure.

I regret my choice of a
window seat
without escape.
The sky is so close to me
and the aisle
feels miles away.

The cheese and onion air
engulfs me in its scent.
This is what hell smells like, I think.
Was I really born into
economy class?
On a budget airline?

Is it too much to ask for
a video screen on
the back of the chair in front?
Is it too much to ask for
a complimentary wine
and a blanket in a plastic bag?

The man beside me offers
a smile and a nod,
his golden grills terrify me.
I fake smile nervously
and sink back
into my *Radio 4* podcast.

These people will spend the next
few days stuffing
their faces with chocolate eggs,
while I am crucified by
their ignorance
and lack of manners.

Jesus told me to be
non-judgemental.
My grandmother
said to always
be myself.
I can't be both.

A Day at the British Library

Today I heard a new song
As my train slow rolled into King's Cross.
Marianne faithfully crooning, deep and rough.
She is London to my open ears.
I never imagined I'd leave here
I never thought I'd forget
to come home, at least twice a year.
Forget I did, and for too long I've been unfed.

Today, opposite Euston,
I saw a woman with intense orange hair.
She tried to brighten up the street of dowdy moving faces.
Only a little sadness in her eyes, she was pushed and pulled by city life;
deflated perhaps. Not beat.

Windrush brought the colonials home
to rebuild England from ground up,
to grow old in a hostile atmosphere
to be sent back when England had enough.
The Black and White News told lies
stirred up pain, violence and mistrust
but the Windrush brought a carnival
of colours and banners and food and love.

Today I saw Anne Frank
in the library, near the lockers.
Built of bronze upon a wooden base
with a beaming smile she offers
a sense of place away from home,
a sense of peace from ghosts of war,
a sense of knowledge from the past
peeking out from behind the wall.

The Insignificance of Mistletoe

Climbing up the oak.
Clinging on.
Contributing nothing to life,
the mistletoe waits.
Waits to play roof to an
uninvited but undenied kiss.
Waits to kill a god through
a cunning brother's trick.
Winter air brings winter nights
and fires filled with rituals and rites.
The mistletoe lingers on the oak.
Waiting still.

The Mess of Tomorrow

"Surely it's only breaking and entering
if you break something. And look
there's a hole in the fence."

So say the voices in my head.

"It's only trespassing if you're not invited
and we asked you here ourselves. Come.
Walk the empty halls."

*Perhaps I'll walk just a little while
until today's world calls.*

"Hear the nurses and the prisoners.
Decide. Is this care?
Or something sinister?"

24

*I love this place, it's magical with
the ivy growing through the walls.*

"Jump over broken floors.
Take your life into your hands
but go careful with your soul."

*I know I shouldn't be here, I know
I could lose my job. What's that? I hear a dog.*

"It's only the living security guard,
ignore him, he'll soon be gone."

*I'll hide in this old bathroom,
I'll rest on broken glass.*

"Look out of that window,
see the grass, see the trees."

Can you hear the birdsong?

"That's the cuckoo and the crow."

Do you see those cats drinking tea?

"They're making the mess of tomorrow."

A London Sonnet

Damn it. It aches to see you again
I'm on your streets just a man. An unknown.
I'm less hungry. I'm a little less vain.
You're scaffold and crane, your skyline has grown.
I see a young man opposite me now,
excited eyes and boyish pink cheeks.
I want to swap places now; I announce
and be in your arms for a few more weeks.

The humming and screeching trains are the same;
there's a dark, hidden joy here always.
There's a joy in my voice speaking your name
I surrender again, I'm lost in your ways.

You chewed me, you spat me, threw me away.
I hope you see now, I'm here anyway.

Humber Bridge

"He came here often before he dived
as the evening sun fell down.
He came here often and memorised
all the waters he'd been around."

These are the words he hears them say,
for now in his head. One day for real.
He hears his mother, his father, his kids,
he hears them crying but what's his is this.

The water in all its muddy depths is
a way away from his daily hell.
It's a way away from the lies he tells
and all the people who "just want to help."

There's one day left to find him here;
sitting lonely above the brown,
watching Vikings from the rails
and going home with no sound.

Virginia's Walk

Parked beside the bridge
turned off the 'War of the Worlds'.
A few other cars close by
—lovers and secret lovers.

Love is far from my mind
listening to the lapping waves.
Hardly any other sound
besides the wind and the owl.

I wonder how she did it,
it must have been so cold.
I wonder if she shivered
with each of her dampened steps.

I come here often.
I wonder if I'll ever walk on;
over the edge and into the lap.
Will she find me?

How long will it take?
Will I hold my breath?
What happens if I change my mind?
Too late to reverse the steps?

I wish I could ask you Virginia.
I wish I could hear you talk.
I wish I could decide if I
will join you, on your walk.

Mirrors

Someone once told me that
pretty boys turn into
bitter men.
I laughed.

Today I look in the mirror,
The years have not been kind.
I hate everyone. I cry.

But then again ...

What are mirrors for?
For evil queens? For
self-portrait artists?

Are they for the vain? Or
the insecure?

Are mirrors for helping
us get lost in ourselves
at the fairground?

They are the greatest of
tricksters. They put Loki to shame.
Telling lies, just close enough to the truth.

You could so easily break them.

Find Me

Find me in the forest.
Find me in a tree.
Pen in my hand.
Paper on my knee.
Listening to birds;
the robin and the crow.

Words on my page,
grow and grow and grow.

Find me in the wind.
Find me in the breeze.
Pen in my hand.
Paper on my knees.
Watching leaves blow;
apples fall to the ground.

Seasons become sentences,
down and down and down.

Find me in the river.
Find me in the sea.
Pen in my hand.
Paper on my knee.
Swimming with dolphins;
beneath what is real.

The sea is a stanza,
on and on and on.

Find me in the coffin.
Find me in the deep.
Pen in my hand.
And paper in my sleep.

Saharan Sand

The sky is filled with Saharan sand.
Dust hovering over the sea
is strange and unnerving.
I can feel the heat of the sun
but have no clue where in the sky she is.

The palms are waving hello, goodbye,
saying "come for a day or stay for a while."
Desert breath hides in the clouds.
I'm not sure yet, if I'll hang around.

A bottle of Rioja and the song
of Spanish voices bring smiles
and memories from my soul.
The gentle salt waves caressing
my feet bring kindness.

Another day is ending.
Tomorrow, tomorrow, come.
Another life so long ago
is gone, is gone, is gone.

Tiki Bar on Fernandina

Talking to my friends at the Tiki Bar on Fernandina, 4,000 miles ago.

I left some things there:
- A kiss on the sand
- A hand on the water
- A shadow in the moonlight
- A whisper on the wind.

What did I whisper? That's between me and the wind.

I brought some things back:
- The moon to protect my shadow
- The water to hold my hand

- The sand to guard my kiss
- The wind in my voice.

Until I Die

There's a high tide warning
in the depths of my heart,
blood pumping and dancing,
the adventure is mine.
I'm going to walk here,
I'm going to run,
I'm going to ride,
Until I crash.

A swell of emotion
is pulling me down,
from the spikes of the bank grass,
to the warmth of the sand.
I'm going to dive here,
I'm going to swim,
I'm going to live,
until I die.

Shard

Pointing triangles to the sky
is our way of saying "Look Up."
The clouds are different every day
but the buildings stay the same.

Pointing triangles to the sky
helps the rain slide down.
Flowing, often heavy, sometimes light
and the paving slabs never change.

Alarm

An alarm is ringing.
On and on, like a demented laser.
I can hear it, but I'm not listening.
I don't know if my neighbours are
being burgled
or murdered;
but I can't get to sleep.

Wildflower

At first, he was a lamb;
springing and alive.
Until he was a rabbit
and knew he had to hide.

Next, he was a raven;
searching for the light.
Until he was an owl,
screeching in the night.

Then he was a wolf;
secure within the pack.
Until he was a tiger,
and roamed his lonely path.

Today he is a Rowan tree;
fixed firmly in the ground.
I am a wildflower, beside him;
silent and unfound.

Cord

It doesn't take long in England
to stray from the beaten track;
to find yourself under woodland cover
and nothing feels better.

You can step out from the city
anytime you choose,
and rest beneath a canopy of green
breathing wild garlic perfume.

Time seems to freeze here,
it holds you, and your thoughts;
like a mother it will feed you
through Earth's umbilical cord.

Next Year

Walking in the last snow of
winter. Ready for the sky to
cover my skin with sun. Soon
my big coat can rest
at last. For now, I let the cold
bite my face and chill my toes.
I let the wind rattle my bones.
Two weeks ago the daffodils were
ready to say hello, today they are
weighed down like monks praying
for a world they will never understand, or ever live in.
Then again, maybe next year.

Museum Assistant on Opening Night

They think they're being all 'arty'
but really, they're just being twits.
They've all rolled up for opening night
—free bubbles and nibbly bits.

The Lord Mayor and his Lady
are dressed up to the nines.
They know a museum private view
brings out the cheese and wine.

The mummy lays in her case of glass
in the centre of the room.
There's reverence as the crowd surrounds her
Thoughts of a curse, that surely looms.

I wish the curse would come attack.
I just want to go back home,
but I'll be here on minimum wage
until opening night is done.

Merlot

An adventure in love begins for me
tonight. I have the Devil's vineyard
in my lonely hands and in my kiss it
lingers like a lost lover—back to play.

A lover can lose appeal—given time,
but this taste of velvet upon my tongue
is enough to me, for an early grave.
I die secure, and safe, in warm
embrace.

Refugee

I'm not from this time,
I'm just hiding;
in this place I can't find
that is riddled with crime.
The blood in my veins is still flowing.

Let me breathe
one more time,
before I cross the borderline.
Out of here, out of sight, out of mind.

'I belong to no man,'
no denying;
any truth behind that lie
doesn't cross my mind.
The pain in my chest is still hurting.

Let me sip
One more time,
to the last one of our kind.
Out of here, out of sight, out of mind.

Opening doors and windows.
Clearing death from the rooms.
We're skeletons playing bingo
locked up in our tombs.

Is it clear?
Are they gone?
Oh—I hope you sing along.
Out of here, out of sight, out of mind.

The Silence

I hear the traffic;
there's always somewhere to go.
I hear the sirens;
Accidents and emergencies
still flow.

I hear the woman next to me;
hacking cough,
she stands in the cold.
I feel the wind on my face
and through my hair.

I feel my eyes close and
my head lower.
My heart beating gratefully.

Thank you. Thank you.
Thank you all.

I see old men in rows;
the boys who returned.
There are lines on their faces;
carved maps of all they've learned.

I see the sky cover the earth
and eyes always watching,
watching, from somewhere.

I am safe in the silence.
Safe and alone,
together with hundreds.
Hundreds unknown.
I dream of a future.
I imagine the past.
I pray to their gods
for the silence to last.

About the Author

Adam Ditchburn was born in Hull, East Yorkshire, in 1982. He spent much of his adult life in London before returning to Yorkshire in 2015, where he lives with his wife and three children. He has worked in a wide range of sectors, including health education, youth work, museums and also spent a year as a pre-novice considering a vocation to religious life. Adam studied both a higher education certificate in theology and a degree in arts and humanities, with a particular focus on creative writing. As a creative artist, Adam has written and performed songs for several years, has released three albums and played widely around the United Kingdom and in the United States.

He has recently shifted his writing focus to prose and poetry. One of his short stories, 'Men Without Ties', was published in the summer 2018 edition of Don Bosco Today magazine. 'As the Crow Flies' is his first collection of printed poems.

Don Bosco Publications is a small Catholic publishing house operated by the Salesians of Don Bosco in the UK.

Saint John Bosco, the founder of the Salesians, believed in the value of books, stating that a good book can become a welcome friend.

As well as publications that include books for clergy, teachers, schools and children, we produce a triannual magazine: Don Bosco Today, and the Salesian calendar once a year.

Further information can be found on our website: www.salesians.org.uk, or Facebook: @donboscopublications.